THE LITTLE MUSTARD BOOK

David Mabey

PIATKUS

Other titles in the series

The Little Green Avocado Book
The Little Garlic Book
The Little Pepper Book
The Little Lemon Book
The Little Apple Book
The Little Strawberry Book
The Little Mushroom Book
The Little Nut Book
The Little Bean Book
The Little Honey Book
The Little Rice Book

© 1984 Judy Piatkus (Publishers) Limited

First published in 1984 by Judy Piatkus
(Publishers) Limited of London

British Library Cataloguing in Publication Data

Mabey, David
  The little mustard book.
  1. Mustard (Condiment)
  I. Title
  641.3′384   TX407.M8

ISBN 0-86188-464-7

Drawings by Linda Broad
Designed by Ken Leeder
Cover photography by John Lee

Typeset by Gilbert Composing Services.
Printed and bound by
The Pitman Press, Bath.

CONTENTS

A POTTED HISTORY
OF MUSTARD

ANCIENT TIMES

The story of mustard begins, appropriately, with mustard seeds. In the earliest times, when hunting and gathering food was still man's main occupation, our ancestors found that chewing handfuls of wild mustard seeds with meat had a pleasant, stimulating effect, often disguising the taste of less than fresh meat. When the first civilized communities appeared in India and Sumeria around 3000 BC, mustard was one of their most useful crops.

Many centuries later, when Belshazzar staged his monumental Babylonian feast, you can be sure that the taste of mustard was on the lips of his guests as they ate and drank the night away, unaware that Darius and the Persian army were about to bring proceedings to an abrupt end. In 336 BC, Darius was involved in a spicy exchange with his rival, Alexander the Great: the Persian sent a bag of sesame seeds to represent the number of his troops, and Alexander replied with a sack of mustard seeds—smaller, perhaps, but more numerous and much more fiery!

The Greeks valued mustard very highly, both as a table condiment and as a wonder drug. However, it was the Romans who exploited mustard's culinary potential to the full. They called mustard *sinapis* and not only sprinkled it over food but ground the seeds in mortars and mixed them with wine, vinegar, oil and honey; they even made exquisite white sauces by adding pine kernels and almonds to this ground paste. Mustard was served with everything from wild boar and udder (stuffed with caraway and salted sea urchin) to sausages and vegetables; it also appeared as an ingredient of many pickles.

MUSTARD IN FRANCE

When the Romans moved into Gaul they took their mustard seeds with them, scattering handfuls along roadsides and over hills. Their knowledge of mustard was eventually inherited by the monasteries; the monks of St Germain des Prés in Paris were famous for producing mustard over a thousand years ago, back in the 10th century.

But it was in the rich wine-growing region of Burgundy that mustard found its real home. And how the people loved it! In 1336, the Duke of Burgundy invited his cousin Philip the Fair, King of

France, to a festival, and while the two men were swapping court gossip their guests were polishing off 70 gallons of mixed mustard during the course of one meal! Mustard was in everyone's thoughts—and on everyone's plate—at that time, from the lowest to the highest in the land: His Holiness Pope John XXII of Avignon, whose devotion to mustard came second only to his devotion to God, was never without it, and even created the title of 'Mustard Maker to the Pope' for an idle nephew who lived in Dijon.

Dijon quickly became the centre of the trade, and it was here that mustard was first pressed into dry tablets. Such was the importance of this condiment that in 1634 laws were passed to grant the men of the town the exclusive rights to make mustard, but in return the privileged citizens had to behave themselves, 'wear clean and sober clothes' and maintain only one shop, so that there could be no argument about the origins of any suspect jar or cask.

The year 1777 was an important one in the history of French mustard, for this was when Monsieur Grey got together with Monsieur Poupon and founded a firm of mustard-makers in Dijon. Grey's secret recipe for a strong mustard made with white wine was manufactured with the help of Poupon's money.

At first the mustard seed was ground laboriously by hand, and it must have been an agonizing task. However, there were rewards. It was said that a tear in the eye of a Dijon mustard-grinder was guaranteed to earn him a bonus; it showed that he was working better, pulverizing the seed more finely than his dry-eyed colleagues! But in 1850 all this came to an end, when the redoubtable Monsieur Grey's mustard-making firm developed the first automatic, steam-operated grinding machine, an invention that subsequently won two medals of honour from the Dijon Academy of Arts, Sciences and Letters.

Mustard-makers have always been good publicists. Alexandre Bornibus, a 19th-century entrepreneur, astutely moved his business from Dijon to fashionable Paris, and was one of the first to employ sandwich-board men to advertise his wares. His vans were the smartest in town and he even packed his 'ladies' mustard' (flavoured with tarragon) in pots made of Sèvres china, adding the catchphrase, 'The contents are worthy of the container.' According to his friend the writer and gastronome Alexandre Dumas (who wrote a classic essay on mustard as a public relations exercise), he invented no fewer than 24 kinds of mustard—as well as 92 types of vinegar!

Dijon is still the centre of French mustard manufacture, responsible for something like 90 per cent of the total produced in the country. Since 1937, Dijon mustard has, like the best wines, been *appellation controlée:* only black or brown seed can be used, and only mustard that conforms to all the legal standards can bear the name of Dijon.

MUSTARD IN ENGLAND

Although mustard grew wild in England, it was not until the arrival of the Romans that mustard-making came into its own. By the Middle Ages it was being ground in little 'querns' or stone handmills, and used as a vital foil to the harsh flavours of salt meat and heavily smoked herrings. By the 13th century there were even authorized 'mustarders' and saucemakers who would mix batches of the condiment for weddings and feasts if the hosts were too lazy. The mustarder ground the seed, blended it with vinegar and packed it into earthenware pots covered with old parchment. According to the medieval writer John Wycliffe it was the practice to use scraps of worthless letters and religious edicts to protect the precious condiment: 'These lettris mai do good for to cover mustard pottis but not thus to wynne men bliss.'

Like the French, the English were prodigious mustard-eaters; and no wonder, when home-grown mustard seed was the cheapest spice on the market, selling for as little as a farthing a pound at the beginning of the 15th century. One of its great uses was as a 'poignant and sharp' sauce to go with brawn.

At the feast marking the enthronement of Archbishop Nevill in 1467, the assembled company sharpened their appetites with 'brawn and mustard, out of course, served with malmsey'. And in the great Tudor households it was the carver's job to see to the mustard and sauces, as well as plying his own special trade. Wynkyn de Worde's *Boke of Kervynge* (1508) recounts in marvellously rich language all that a well-respected man of the knife should know, including how to 'sauce him with poudres of gynger, mustarde, vynegre and salte'.

In the 17th century, Tewkesbury mustard was all the rage, and the herbalist Coles, writing in 1657, noted that 'In Glostershire about Teuxbury they grind Mustard seed and make it up into balls which are brought to London and other remote places as being the best that the world affords.' Mustard balls were made from local wild mustard often ground with a 'cannon bullet'. The powdered mustard was then dampened, pressed into balls and dried hard. When needed they were diluted with vinegar, apple juice, cider, buttermilk or even cherry juice.

The sound of millstones grinding, and the 'angry thunder' of cannon balls against iron mortars gave mustard-making a demonic aspect, and the resulting mustard flour was coarse-grained and speckled in appearance. But around 1720, a certain Mrs Clements, who lived in Saddler Street, Durham, perfected an entirely new method of producing mustard flour. By pounding and sieving the seed she found a way of obtaining a fine yellow flour free from bits of husk, and she travelled the country on a packhorse selling her invention, but kept the method a secret! She even found favour with King George I, and was soon a household name throughout the land.

Mrs Clements' secret died with her, but in 1742 Messrs Keens of Garlick Hill, London, set up a factory to produce mustard in a similar style. It is tempting to think that their name was immortalized to make the phrase 'as keen as mustard'. Then, in 1814, a young Norfolk miller named Jeremiah Colman moved into the water-mill at Stoke Holy Cross, near Norwich, and set in motion the most famous name in English mustard since the cunning lady of Durham. His factory thundered to the sound

of whole batteries of pestles and mortars grinding and pulverizing; the fine mustard flour was then sieved through specially woven silk to remove the coarse bran. Colman's rapidly became synonymous with English mustard in its new form. Today they still dominate the market, although there has been a shift of fashion since the 1970s with the rise of small enterprises like Gordon's and Wiltshire Tracklements (Urchfont Mustard), who make a whole range of English coarse-grained mustards.

THE ART OF
MUSTARD-MAKING:
'SOME NOTABLE
HISTORICAL
RECEIPTS'

'Carefully clean mustard seed and sift, then wash in cold water and when well washed leave for two hours in the water. Then remove, press it with your hands and put in a new or a thoroughly cleaned mortar, and pound it with a pestle. When it is pounded, put the mash into the middle of the mortar and compress it with the flat of your hand. Next, when you have pressed it, scarify it and after having placed a few glowing coals on it, pour water mixed with cooking soda on it, in order to remove all bitterness and paleness. Immediately after, lift the mortar so that all the moisture may be drained away. After this add strong wine vinegar, mix with the pestle and strain. The juice is very good to spice turnips. If, by the way, you want to prepare mustard for use at the table, when you have squeezed it out add pine-kernels which should be as fresh as possible and almonds, pound carefully and pour vinegar on ... This mustard is not only suitable as sauce, but is even good to look at, for it is of extreme whiteness when made carefully.'

Columella, *De re rustica*, 42 AD

'Take the mustard seed, and grind one and a half pints of it with honey, and Spanish oil, and make it into a liquid sauce with vinegar ... To make mustard for the pot, slice some horseradish, and lay it to soak in vinegar, squeezing it well, and add a lump of sugar and an onion chopt. Use the vinegar from this mixture to mix the mustard.'

John Evelyn, *Acetaria,* 1699

'To make Jesuits' Mustard'
'Thoroughly mix ten sardines, a quarter of a pound of ground brown mustard, three-quarters of a pound of ground white mustard, and two hundred capers. Make into a paste with about a quart of boiling vinegar.'

The Still Room by Mrs Charles Roundell and Harry Roberts, Bodley Head, 1913

'To make Mustard as at Dusseldorf'
'Take two earthenware pans, and place in each a quart of vinegar. In one place a quarter of an ounce of thyme leaves, and in the other place three minced onions. Let them stand for forty-eight hours. Bruise half a pound of white mustard seed and half a pound of black mustard seed, and put them in a pan with a tea-spoonful of powdered cloves, a tea-spoonful of powdered coriander, half a pound of salt, and the strained vinegar. Thoroughly mix. Add a little more vinegar if the mixture is too thick, or a little more mustard if it is too thin. Parsley, celery, or other herbs may be used instead of onions to flavour the vinegar.'

Ibid

THE NAMING OF MUSTARD

The Romans used to produce what they called *mustum ardens* or 'burning must' by fermenting mustard seeds in grape juice, and this is the most likely derivation of the word 'mustard'.

Most of the words for mustard, at least in Western languages, come from this, or from *sinapis*, the Latin word for the mustard plant: French: *moutarde;* Spanish: *mostaza;* Italian: *senape* (the word *mostarda* is usually reserved for the conserve known as *mostarda di Cremona,* see page 55); German: *senf;* Danish: *sennep.*

MUSTARD PLANTS

The mustard we use as a condiment is derived from the seeds of three species of plants from the *Cruciferae* family, so its relatives are household names like Brussels sprouts, cauliflower and turnips, while its cousins include watercress and wallflowers.

BLACK MUSTARD (*Brassica nigra*) originated in the Middle East and Asia, but has been cultivated in Europe for hundreds of years. It is an annual that produces masses of distinctive yellow flowers during

June. By August these have given way to cylindrical pods with ribs and a seedless beak; the seeds themselves, arranged in rows, are actually dark reddish-brown in colour.

The seeds of black mustard, with their bite and pungency, were used almost universally until the 1930s, but they did not find favour with commercial growers. *B.nigra* was a huge rangy plant, often growing to twice the height of a man, and with the irritating habit of shedding its seeds without warning. In a word, it was unruly. It had to be harvested by hand and scythed down like overgrown wheat by a small army of workers. To judge by old photographs of labourers in the mustard fields of Norfolk at the turn of the century, it must have been an extraordinary spectacle. But English agriculture has changed since then, and *B.nigra* is no longer cultivated to the same degree. Only in the peasant farming communities of Southern Italy, Sicily and Ethiopia might you still see a harvest in the old style.

BROWN MUSTARD (*Brassica juncea*) was developed by growers as a manageable alternative to *B.nigra*. Its French name *(moutarde de Chine)* and Spanish name *(mostaza de Indias)* remind us of the plant's oriental origins, although it is now grown widely in parts of England and Northern Europe. The great advantage of *B. juncea* is its shortness when compared to *B. nigra* and its neat ordered growth, which means that it can be harvested by machine. Otherwise it is little different to *B. nigra*, although it does lack some of that uncompromising pungency. People who complain that mustard has lost its kick and 'isn't what it used to be' can find the answer in the demise of *B. nigra*.

These days, most mustard-makers—especially large producers like Colman's—use *B. juncea*, although many smaller enterprises such as Wiltshire Tracklements (Urchfont Mustard) still proudly make their condiments with black mustard.

WHITE MUSTARD (*Sinapis alba*) is a native of the Mediterranean and a close relative of the wild charlock (*S. arvensis*). It is now grown particularly in the eastern counties of England and in the USA, and like other mustard plants it is a yellow-flowered annual. But its seed pods are quite unmistakable: they are bulbous and hairy, have broad flattened beaks and contain only three or four large yellowish seeds.

White mustard has little or no pungency, but it does provide its own distinctive qualities when blended with black or brown mustard. It is used a great deal in English mustards and it is the main ingredient of American mustards, but its use is forbidden in the ancient stronghold of French mustard, Dijon.

THE CONSTITUENTS OF MUSTARD

The outer husks of mustard seeds contain a good deal of mucilage (a sticky, gum-like substance), but it is the cotyledons which house the plant's most important substances. As well as about 30 per cent of a fixed oil consisting of glycerides of various acids (mainly oleic, stearic, erucic and brassic), separate cells contain a crystalline glucoside (sinigrin in black mustard, sinalbin in white) and an enzyme called myrosin. When crushed mustard seeds are mixed with water, the enzyme brings together the glucoside and water, forming a volatile oil that gives mustard its characteristic pungency. The oil from black mustard is more pungent than that from white.

Ripe mustard seeds do not contain any starch, although some brands of prepared powder do have added flour.

When mustard seeds are pressed, a valuable *fatty* oil, rich in trace elements, is produced.

GROWING MUSTARD SPROUTS

The young seedlings of white mustard *(Sinapis alba)* are grown and eaten as a salad vegetable; they are the 'mustard' in 'mustard and cress'. They can be grown right through the year in a heated greenhouse, where the temperature is 50–60°F, or in small batches in a warm kitchen.

In the greenhouse, simply fill some seed trays with fine sandy soil, water well and then sprinkle the mustard seeds evenly over the surface. Firm them in but don't cover with soil. Cover the trays with wood or cloth and leave for a few days until the seeds have germinated. Then remove the cover and expose to the light, so that the yellow leaves of the seedlings turn green. Once the sprouts are 2 to 3 inches high they are ready for cutting. If you want a continuous supply, simply sow a batch of seeds every week.

In the kitchen you can grow the seeds on a piece of wet flannel or blotting paper. Cover, keep moist and put in a warm place until germination occurs. Then proceed as above.

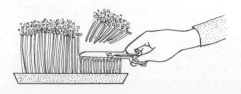

THE INGREDIENTS OF PREPARED MUSTARD

In the very beginning mustard was eaten neat, but it was not long before extra ingredients were added: liquids to turn it into a paste and herbs and spices to make it more interesting. But poor ingredients make awful mustard, and the condiment was not immune to the pernicious practices of adulteration when there was little or no control over what was sold.

Sir Hugh Plat in his *Delightes for Ladies* (1605), had this to say: 'Our mustard which we buy from the Chandlers at this day is many times made up with vile and filthy vinegar such as our stomack would abhor if we should see it before the mixing thereof with the seeds.'

And more than two centuries later, food-faking was still big business, to such an alarming degree that the medical journal *The Lancet* took on the role of a 19th-century consumer guide, and between 1851 and 1854 produced a series of reports on various foodstuffs. Its team of Scientific Detective Police (as *Punch* nicknamed them) collared 33 samples of mustard and found only four that were genuine; the worst offender (sample number 27) was condemned as an 'injurious combination'. Colman's were quick to give themselves a pat on the back in public, and pointed out that two of the genuine samples were their own, and that 'in their Pure Mustards nothing that known skill and improved machinery can obtain from finest seed remains unsecured, and, whether for prompt and specific medical effects, or as a table condiment, these Mustards are equally valuable'.

We may not need to worry about adulteration these days, although mustard-hunters should take the time to read the list of ingredients on any new brand they discover; artificial additives in the form of colouring, flavouring and preservatives are the things to avoid.

The main ingredients of today's prepared mustards are as follows. More specific details can be gleaned from pages 19–29.

WATER: Traditionally the medium for mixing English mustard.

WINE, WINE VINEGAR AND VERJUICE: Wine features in many French mustards, and the choice can vary from the unfermented claret used for Bordeaux mustard to the sharp Aligoté white wine from Burgundy that distinguishes Amora mustard. Various vinegars appear in almost all Continental and American mustards (sometimes in conjunction with wine). Verjuice (green grape juice) is used only occasionally these days.

CIDER AND CIDER VINEGAR: Popular in many of the new English mustards.

BEER: 'Real ale' mustards make use of some of England's best brews.

SALT: The essential seasoning.

FLOUR: Wheat flour is used in some English mustards; it improves the characteristics of the powder by absorbing some of the natural oiliness of the mustard seed. In countries like America, laws prevent the inclusion of flour in mustard.

SUGAR AND HONEY: Sugar provides the sweetness for Bavarian and Scandinavian mustard in particular, while honey is a favourite ingredient of new mustards from small firms in Wales and Scotland.

SPICES: There is an increasingly forthright use of spices in mustard. Allspice, chillies and black peppercorns are the commonest, not to mention Madagascan green peppercorns and at least one mustard with fennel seeds. Turmeric is used to boost the yellow colour of mustard.

HORSERADISH: There is an age-old affinity between horseradish and mustard (the 16th-century herbalist, John Gerard, wrote that horseradish 'is commonly used for sauce to eate fish with and such meates as we do mustarde'). Today's Tewkesbury mustard is always made with horseradish, although not every historical recipe bears out this connection.

HERBS: Tarragon is the classic mustard herb, appearing in everything from Bordeaux to Dusseldorf mustard. In England, Colman's have recently added a chive mustard, a tarragon and thyme mustard and a horseradish mustard to their range. In France, Maille produce an extraordinary 'mustard with green herbs' that has to be seen to be believed: it is as green as its name. And if you are looking for a real curiosity, seek out a wonderful French mustard with nettle leaves.

OTHER FLAVOURINGS: These include lemon juice, lime juice, orange peel, sesame seeds, black olives, celery, tomatoes, and beetroot . . . to name but a few!

MUSTARD STATISTICS

* By far the largest mustard grower in the world is Canada, with about 250,000 acres devoted to the crop. France and Germany come next, followed by the UK, with something over 10,000 acres (mainly in the fertile counties of Eastern England).

* According to the most recent figures, issued in 1980, the country with the largest mustard market is the USA, with a staggering annual total of 198,000 tonnes; France is next with 44,400, then Germany 37,725, the UK 9,000, Canada 7,900 and Belgium 7,500.

  These figures give a useful picture since the mustard market in most countries is steady or growing very slowly. (Note: 1 tonne or metric ton = 1,000 Kg)

* The Americans also consume more mustard per head than anyone else. In 1980 the figures were: USA 915 grams per person per year (the equivalent of almost ten 4oz [100 gram] jars), France 836, followed by Switzerland, Belgium, Sweden and Germany in that order. The UK is well down this list, with only 161 grams per person.

TYPES AND BRANDS OF MUSTARD

Mustard is a condiment for all occasions, and its place on the side of the plate is unchallenged by any other sauce, relish or seasoning. Nothing is so useful, so versatile, or so effective at complementing other foods while contributing its own distinctive qualities.

Of course fondness for mustard is a very personal matter, and everyone has his own special favourite, a mustard that is irreplaceable. (King Louis XI of France was such a man: he loved one particular

mustard so much that he used to carry a little pot around with him, just in case there was none on hand where he was dining!)

The following catalogue of mustards is not fully comprehensive; such is the interest in mustard that new ones are appearing all the time. So there are always discoveries to be made, and mustard-hunters are urged to keep their eyes open.

The list is broadly divided into English, French, German and American mustards, as these are the most important and readily available. But good mustard is also made in Belgium, Holland, Switzerland, Austria and Poland. A lot of mustard is made and eaten in Scandinavia, too, and it is worth noting Danish *fiskesennep* or fish mustard: Danish fishmongers always have a bucket of this on hand, from which customers can take a ladleful; it is made from coarsely-ground brown and white seeds with salt and vinegar (the mild Danish kind made from molasses). There is also an exceedingly rare and lethally hot mustard which comes from China.

ENGLISH MUSTARD

There has been a real renaissance in English mustard since the mid-1970s. Until then, it was traditionally a blend of finely powdered black (or brown) seeds, judiciously mixed with white seeds and a little wheat flour. But fashions have changed, and alongside the familiar yellow powder and smooth paste, there's now a whole range of new coarse-grained mustards made with wine, vinegar, cider and beer, rather than water.

COLMAN'S MUSTARD

For more than 150 years, the Norwich firm of Colman's has been the most famous name in English mustard, and there's no better way of seeing how it all developed than to visit Colman's Mustard Shop, Bridewell Alley, Norwich, Norfolk: a splendid Victorian-style emporium dedicated to the condiment.

Colman's greatest mustard is the dry powder known as Genuine Double Superfine. Mixed with water and allowed to bloom into flavour, it is traditional English mustard at its glorious best. It is no accident that Colman's use as their emblem a bull's head, for their mustard is superb with roast beef; it also highlights some of England's finest foods: Melton Mowbray pork pies, Bury black puddings, faggots, brawn, chops, steaks, kidneys, bacon and, of course, sausages.

As well as mustard in powder form, Colman's also manufacture prepared English mustards of various strengths and flavours, plus their versions of German, American and French mustards.

TAYLOR'S MUSTARD

Since 1832, Taylor's of Newport Pagnell, Buckinghamshire, have been producing fine English mustard in the traditional way from mustard flour, wheat flour, salt and turmeric, and have maintained a healthy independent reputation. Their Original Prepared Mustard is just as it should be—sharp, hot and pungent.

TEWKESBURY MUSTARD

James Bennett in the *History of Tewkesbury* (1830) noted that 'good housewives uniformly pound the mustard in an iron mortar with a large cannon ball and having carefully sifted the flour, mix it with a cold infusion of horseradish and beat it well for at least an hour.'

Most of today's Tewkesbury mustard (produced without cannon balls!) is marketed by a London firm called *La Favorite.* It is pale and smooth, with a hint of Dijon about it (the recipe now includes wine vinegar rather than water), and with flakes of horseradish adding a distinctive bite.

'His wit is as thick as Tewkesbury mustard: there is no more conceit in him than in a mallet.'

Shakespeare, *Henry IV Part 2*

URCHFONT MUSTARD
(Wiltshire Tracklements)

The word 'tracklements' (meaning garnishes or accompaniments) has the ring of old cottage English about it, and William Tullberg's business has all the spirit of cottage industry at its best.

Tullberg produces four coarse-grained mustards. Black and white seeds are his raw materials, and they are barely crushed during the grinding process in order to keep their volatile oils intact. Top of the list is the Full Strength, a powerful condiment tailor-made for Wiltshire's hams, sausages and pies; Urchfont Black is strongly aromatic due to its high proportion of black seed; subtly flavoured Tarragon Mustard is ideal for salad dressings and mayonnaise, while Honey Mustard is recommended with pork, veal and chicken.

Two fine-ground mustards (one with traditional West Country cider, the other with local beer) plus four grades of pure dry mustard powder (*without* added flour) complete the picture.

GORDON'S MUSTARD

Charles Gordon of Surrey also produces a splendid range of mustards, but uses the old method of stone-grinding the seed, which produces a much finer texture.

English Vineyard Mustard—his best known product—is flavoured with English wine; pungent Green Peppercorn Mustard is the obvious choice with steak; English Farmhouse Mustard, lightly flavoured with cider vinegar, goes well with pork and ham, while the Real Ale Mustard is a robust accompaniment to anything from sausages to braised oxtail; crunchy Wholegrain Mustard is recommended for barbecues, and there is also a smooth Strong English Mustard.

Several wholegrain honey mustards are produced in Scotland and Wales by firms like the Arran Mustard Company, Scotts of Carluke (who have been in business since 1880) and Cambrian Mustard.

Crabtree & Evelyn, Elsenham, Wilsons and St Elven in Cornwall also produce mustard, and more brands are appearing all the time.

FRENCH MUSTARD

Although powdered mustard was produced in Dijon before the 17th century, French mustards today are always mixed, and are broadly divided into three types: sharp clean-tasting Dijon, dark spicy Bordeaux and a range of old-style coarse-grained mustards, including *Moutarde de Meaux*.

GREY-POUPON MUSTARD

The classic *moutarde au vin blanc* is made by pre-soaking black or brown mustard seeds, grinding the resultant porridge with white wine, salt and spices, and filtering out the husks on the way. The final product is pale, smooth, sharp and strong. It is unsurpassed as an ingredient for sauces, salad dressings and mayonnaise; it is ideal for eating with dishes such as steak, where the taste of the food must not be masked, and it makes the perfect accompaniment to chicken, veal, turkey, salads and vegetables.

Like Colman's, Grey-Poupon has its own shop at 32, rue de la Liberté in Dijon. Here you can see marvellous antique jars with hand-painted wording on them, alongside present-day versions.

MAILLE MUSTARD

Dating back to 1747, this firm produces a number of mustards including *moutarde à l'ancienne* (old-style mustard), a very concentrated, coarse-grained condiment made with diluted white wine. Also there is a classic Dijon mustard, a mild sweet mustard, a vivid-green herb mustard and an extraordinarily colourful *moutarde des trois fruits rouges*, which is bright red and includes beetroot among its ingredients.

AMORA MUSTARD

This large Dijon firm is noted for its strong coarse-grained mustard, made with sharp Aligoté Burgundy white wine.

DELOUIS MUSTARD

Delouis fils of Champsac produce the fanciest of all French mustards. Their formidable selection includes mustards with celery, lemon, green peppercorns, pink 'peppercorns', black olives, cider vinegar, sherry vinegar, mixed herbs, Limousin red wine, fennel seeds and, most unexpected of all, nettle leaves.

BORDEAUX MUSTARD

Until quite recently, if an Englishman asked for 'French mustard' this is what he wanted. Bordeaux mustard, made with unfermented claret, was originally shipped over to England with consignments of prestigious Bordeaux wine. It is dark because it contains finely-ground husk, and is flavoured with sugar, spices and tarragon.

Bordeaux mustard does not have the clean flavour or usefulness of its Burgundian rivals, but it is pleasantly mild and good with cold meats or sausages.

MOUTARDE DE MEAUX

The French have always had the knack of presenting and packaging their mustard attractively, and *Moutarde de Meaux* comes in wide-mouthed stoneware jars corked and sealed with red wax. The story of the mustard is printed in archaic lettering on the label: originally made by monks of the ancient order of Meaux, and a royal favourite since 1632,

Moutarde de Meaux was acquired by the Pommery family in 1760, and they duly kept the secrets of the recipe intact.

To describe this delicate product as a coarse-grained mustard with roughly crushed seeds in a paste does not really do it justice. In fact it is one of the few mustards that can be happily eaten on its own; if you want to serve it as a condiment, pick some bland, simple food that will not mask its marvellous flavour.

Other brands worth looking out for include Theveniaud (established in Dijon in 1840, and trading under the name of *L'Incomparable*); Fallot from the great Burgundian city of Beaune; *Moutarde Florida* from Champagne, and *Olida*, made in Yvetot, Normandy.

GERMAN MUSTARD

The Germans are the world's greatest sausage makers (one of their proudest boasts is that they produce no fewer than 1,500 different types), so it is only natural that they should be mustard-makers— and eaters—too.

DUSSELDORF MUSTARD

For many years Dusseldorf has been almost synonymous with German mustard. One well-known firm, Frenzel, has been in business since 1903, although the trade is obviously much older than that. Frenzel produce a delicious herb mustard—pale, sharp-tasting, finely ground and speckled with herbs—which goes perfectly with chicken and fish. There is also a darker-toned Superfine blend that is rich and spicy like a Bordeaux mustard and is best eaten with foods such as steak, bacon and game. The people of Dusseldorf like their mustard with *'halber Hahn'*, literally 'half a chicken', but actually a kind of cheese roll!

BAVARIAN MUSTARD

A very distinctive, mild, sweet mustard that is finely ground but still retains a certain graininess due to bits of husk. This delicate condiment is obligatory with the renowned 'white' veal sausages (Münchener weisswurst) of the region, complementing rather than smothering their fine flavour. Whether the sausages are lightly steamed or served grilled with sauerkraut and potato purée, locals insist that Bavarian mustard should be on the plate. A good brand is Kühne of Hamburg.

TAFELSENF

Literally 'table mustard', this is the useful, everyday condiment for grills, roasts, cold meats and sausages—including the famous frankfurter. Many firms like Meica and Hengstenberg produce this medium-hot, smooth yellow mustard, which is not unlike our own in character.

The firm of Aromac in Hamelin pack their mustard in glass beer mugs vividly decorated with birds and flowers. So, after the mustard is all gone you can at least console yourself with one of the country's hoppy brews!

AMERICAN MUSTARD

Think of American mustard and you think of hot-dogs; together they're an inseparable double act. But they were not always such a hit: in *Happy Days*, H.L. Mencken didn't mince words when he wrote, 'I devoured hot-dogs in Baltimore back in 1886 . . . They contained precisely the same rubbery, indigestible pseudo-sausage that millions of Americans now eat, and they leaked the same flabby, puerile mustard.'

But hot-dogs, and mustard, survived this assault, and Americans are now the most prodigious mustard-eaters in the world. The mustard they squeeze over their hot-dogs is a jazzy, technicolour condiment—bright yellow, thick, mild and intended to be used lavishly. One firm, R.T. French, whose address is 1, Mustard Street, Rochester, New York, sell their mustard with the slogan 'Spread a little sunshine', and their range includes not only a pure mustard, but a brown spicy one, a horseradish version and something called Onion Bits, which is more like a chunky relish. Like all American mustards they are made entirely from white mustard seed *(S. alba)*, mixed with vinegar, salt, turmeric and spices.

American mustard is particularly useful in sauces, as well as for flavouring dressings and mayonnaise to go with eggs, tuna and coleslaw.

MIXING MUSTARD

Most mustards come ready-mixed, but English mustard is different. It is also available as a dry powder that can be made up quickly and easily whenever it is needed.

The secret of success lies in understanding the various constituents of mustard, and how they react. (See also page 13). When mustard seeds are crushed and mixed with water, the myrosin enzyme and glucoside contained in the seeds forms a volatile oil which gives mustard its characteristic pungency.

But, like all enzymes, myrosin needs time to work and is easily upset. Boiling water 'kills' it, leaving the mustard full of unconverted glucoside, which is unpleasantly bitter.

So when mixing mustard, proceed as follows: blend the powder with *cold* water, added a little at a time, and stir well until a thick, smooth paste is formed; leave for at least 10 minutes so that the full flavour can develop.

Whatever you do, don't follow in the footsteps of the great Charles Francatelli, chef to Queen Victoria, who recommended mixing dry mustard in a teacup with boiling water in his *Plain Cookery Book for the Working Classes* (1852), a philanthropic work written for the less fortunate souls beyond the palace gates.

Although water is the obvious choice for mixing mustard, you can try using milk and enriching the condiment with a little cream. Our ancestors, often more adventurous than ourselves, made use of grape or apple juice, cider, wine or buttermilk when mixing mustard.

Once the mustard has been mixed, and the volatile oil formed, you can safely add salt and acid substances such as vinegar, if you wish.

Mixed mustard loses its flavour and character after a few hours, so it should be made in small batches when needed. On the other hand, dry mustard powder will keep well, provided it does not become damp.

MAKING MUSTARD AT HOME

If you have an adventurous spirit, it is worth trying to make your own mustard. You will not need any special equipment and it is great fun. I have outlined one method, but this is only intended to give general guidelines; experiment with different blends of black and white seed, vary the grinding to create a range of textures, and try out lots of different herbs, spices and flavourings.

Obtain your mustard seed from a seed merchant, wholefood shop or delicatessen that sells spices in bulk.

Use a coffee grinder for finely ground mustard (make sure you clean it well after use) and a pestle and mortar for rougher, coarse-grained textures. Or try a combination of both.

Make small amounts of mustard at a time until you have perfected a formula.

METHOD

1. Use a mixture of black (or brown) and white seed: try equal amounts to begin with, and vary the proportions later to suit your taste. Grind the seed in a coffee grinder or pound roughly using a pestle and mortar.
2. Put the seed into a large stoneware or glass storage jar and moisten with water.
3. Add enough white wine vinegar just to cover the seed, plus a little salt and your choice of seasonings: honey, crushed green peppercorns, sesame seeds, tarragon, freshly ground black peppercorns, allspice and chilli powder are some that are commonly used.
4. Cover the jar and allow to steep for up to a week at room temperature.
5. Drain off any excess liquor, give the mustard a stir and cover the jar securely. Store in a cool place. The mustard should keep for up to six months before opening. Once opened use quickly.

COOKING WITH MUSTARD

* Choose the right mustard for the job. There are no hard and fast rules, so be guided by the fieriness of the mustard and its ingredients. Use plain rather than fancy mustards unless you want a very specific flavour to emerge.

* Mustard will impart its own colour to a sauce. Pale mustards like Dijon tend to be the most useful for saucemaking.

* Use coarse-grained mustards if you want a rough texture, e.g. for spreading over steaks. Their speckled appearance can also add a new dimension to a dish.

* If you are using honey mustard, remember that it may caramelize if it is heated too strongly.

* In general, add mustard late and cook gently. Like pepper, it depends on volatile oils for its special pungency, and these are easily lost during cooking.

* And finally, before the recipes, a cheering note for slimmers: Dijon mustard has only 15 calories per tablespoon!

MUSTARD RECIPES

PARSNIP AND MUSTARD SOUP

A wholesome but subtly-flavoured soup which comes courtesy of William Tullberg.

2 large parsnips
1 onion
1 clove garlic
2 oz butter
2 teaspoons Urchfont Black Mustard
1 pint chicken stock
salt and pepper
cream or parsley, to garnish

Peel and grate the parsnips, onion and garlic as finely as possible and fry in the butter until the onions have become transparent. Stir in the Urchfont mustard. Boost the heat for a few minutes, then add the chicken stock (a good stock cube is perfectly acceptable). Liquidize, then cook gently for 20 minutes, adding salt and pepper to taste.

Serve hot with a swirl of cream or cold with fresh chopped parsley.

Serves 4

CRAB LOUIS

Created by the chef at the Olympic Club, Seattle, USA, this salad was a favourite of the great tenor, Caruso, when he was touring with the Metropolitan Opera Company. Apparently he kept ordering it until there was none left in the kitchen.

The addition of Dijon mustard to the classic recipe has a suitably harmonious effect.

2 tablespoons mayonnaise
2 teaspoons chilli sauce
1 teaspoon Dijon mustard
1 onion, finely chopped
shredded lettuce
8 oz fresh crabmeat
hard-boiled eggs, tomatoes and avocado pear,
   to garnish

Make a dressing by combining the mayonnaise, chilli sauce, mustard and chopped onion. Mix well and chill.

Shred the lettuce, arrange on a large plate and top with the fresh crabmeat. Garnish with sliced hard-boiled eggs, pieces of tomato and sliced avocado pear. Pour the dressing over the salad and serve.

Serves 2

MONKFISH THERMIDOR

Classically this dish is made with lobster, but good versions can be prepared using scampi, prawns, crayfish or monkfish.

Sauce:
$\frac{1}{2}$ oz butter
$\frac{1}{2}$ oz flour
$\frac{1}{2}$ pint stock
1 tablespoon chopped shallot
3 tablespoons white wine
1 teaspoon Dijon mustard

2 lb monkfish
1 oz butter
2 oz diced mushrooms
chopped parsley, to garnish

To make the sauce, melt the butter and stir in the flour to form a roux; pour in the hot stock, stirring well, and allow to cook slowly for 20 minutes.

Meanwhile cook the chopped shallot in the white wine until the latter is reduced by half. Strain and stir into the sauce, with the mustard. Keep warm.

Chop the monkfish into pieces and sauté lightly in the butter with diced mushrooms for 3–4 minutes until the fish is firm. Add the sauce, garnish with chopped parsley and serve with rice.

Serves 4 as a first course; 2 as a main course

STILTON SOUFFLÉ

This tasty soufflé is a good way of using up a surfeit of Stilton cheese, and can be served as either a first course or, at the end of a meal, as a savoury.

4 oz Stilton cheese
3 eggs, separated
1 oz butter
1 tablespoon flour
1 teaspoon Colman's mustard (mixed)
¼ pint milk
salt and pepper
a pinch of cayenne pepper

Crumble the Stilton. Beat the egg yolks until smooth. Melt the butter in a saucepan and blend in the flour and the mustard. Gradually add the milk, stirring well over a low heat until the mixture is thick and smooth; add the Stilton and simmer, stirring until the cheese has melted. Remove from heat and allow to cool for 2 minutes. Beat in the egg yolks slowly; season with salt, pepper and cayenne to taste.

Whip the egg whites until stiff and fold them into the prepared soufflé mixture. Grease 4 individual soufflé dishes (or one large one), and bake in a hot, pre-heated oven at 400°F (200°C), Gas Mark 6 for 20 minutes (allow 10 minutes extra for a large soufflé).

The soufflés should be well-risen, crisp and golden on the outside, soft and moist inside.

Serves 4

WELSH RAREBIT

Some call it 'rarebit', others know it as 'rabbit', but everyone agrees that it is Welsh. In fact, it seems that citizens of the Principality would give up almost anything for a taste of their favourite dish: Andrew Boorde, the 16th-century master of physic and guru of 'dietary health', recounted a curious tale concerning Welshmen who were lured away from the gates of paradise, no less, by the irresistible cries of 'Roysty'd chese!'

Of course there is a world of difference between 'cheese on toast' and a true rarebit made with cheese, ale and mustard.

½ oz butter
8 oz Cheddar cheese, grated
2 fl oz ale
1 teaspoon prepared English mustard
salt and pepper
4 slices toast

Melt the butter in a pan and add the grated cheese. Blend well until the cheese is melted. Add the ale, mustard, salt and pepper. Pour the mixture piping hot over buttered toast, put under the grill to brown, and serve straight away as the topping bubbles.

Topped with a couple of poached eggs, this becomes Buck Rarebit; a slice of ham also makes a delicious topping.

Serves 4

SKEWERED SCHINKENWURST

Schinkenwurst is a German ham sausage smoked over beech and ash to which juniper berries have been added. It can be sliced into chunks and used for these spicy kebabs.

4 tablespoons German mustard (e.g. Aromac)
2 tablespoons chopped fresh dill
2 tablespoons cooking oil
12 oz schinkenwurst cut into chunks
½ cucumber
4 rashers smoked streaky bacon
4 small tomatoes, cut in half
1 oz butter

Blend the mustard and fresh dill with the oil. Slice the schinkenwurst and cucumber into ½ inch thick chunks and marinade in the oil mixture for 1 hour. Cut the rind off the bacon, cut rashers in half and make into 8 rolls. Thread sausages pieces, cucumber, tomato and bacon rolls alternately on to 4 skewers. Brush with melted butter and grill for 15 minutes, turning frequently.

Serves 4

SAUTÉED KIDNEYS WITH MUSTARD AND WINE

A quick and tasty luncheon dish; serve with rice or croûtons of fried bread to soak up the sauce.

12 lambs' kidneys
3 oz butter
1 onion, finely chopped
¼ pint dry white wine
1 tablespoon lemon juice
1 tablespoon Dijon mustard
chopped parsley to garnish

Skin the kidneys, remove any fat, core, but keep whole. Sauté in 2 oz butter for 5 minutes, turning frequently until firm and slightly brown. Do not overcook. Remove to a hot dish and keep warm. Add the onion to the pan, fry gently until transparent, then stir in the white wine and lemon juice. Cook fiercely until the liquid has reduced by half. Blend the mustard with the remaining butter and add to the pan, off the heat, stirring in a spoonful at a time. Slice the kidneys, return to pan, and toss over a low heat for a couple of minutes. Decorate with freshly chopped parsley and serve.

Serves 4

PORK WITH APRICOT STUFFING

This is a feast of a dish. The recipe is reproduced by kind permission of Colman's of Norwich.

Stuffing:

6 oz dried apricots
½ oz butter
2 medium onions, finely chopped
3 oz breadcrumbs
1 dessertspoon grated lemon rind, and the juice of
  1 lemon
1 teaspoon dried rosemary
1 level teaspoon Colman's mustard powder
salt and pepper

5 lb pork loin, boned and ready for stuffing
2 teaspoons mustard powder

Barely cover the apricots with cold water, bring to the boil and simmer for 5 minutes. Remove the apricots and cut them into strips. Melt the butter in a pan and sauté the onions until soft. Mix the onion, apricot strips and the breadcrumbs together. Add the lemon rind and juice, rosemary and mustard. Season well.

Stuff the joint and secure firmly with string or a skewer. Rub all over with mustard powder—this ensures a crisp and well flavoured crackling. Roast for 2 hours at 400°F (200°C), Gas Mark 6, basting occasionally with the pan juices.

Serves 6 generously

DEVILLED CHICKEN

The technique of devilling was, in Victorian times, a way of revitalizing the remains of cold joints and game birds by spicing them with a fiery mixture and searing them under the grill. These days, devilled chicken is the obvious choice, although turkey, pheasant, rabbit and pork are equally good. And if you are playing host to a gathering of hard-drinking revellers, why not offer them a dish of devilled *mixed* meats!

4 cooked chicken joints (or other meat of your choice)
2 oz mango chutney
1 tablespoon Worcestershire sauce
1 teaspoon cayenne pepper
2 teaspoons English or Dijon mustard
melted butter, for basting

Skin the chicken joints and make several slits in the meat. Mix the chutney, Worcestershire sauce, cayenne pepper and mustard to a paste and rub well into the meat. Put under a hot grill, baste with melted butter and turn so that an even crust forms. Heat through and serve.

Serves 4

ROAST RABBIT

A delicious way of cooking young rabbit. It is an interesting recipe because the mustard is not added at the end of the cooking, but at the beginning, so that its flavour can permeate the meat.

2 young rabbits
6 oz Dijon mustard
1 lb streaky bacon
black pepper
2 oz butter

Ask your butcher to prepare and truss the rabbits ready for roasting. Spread thickly with a coating of mustard and wrap up completely in thin rashers of bacon. Season with pepper and lay the rabbits on a rack in a roasting pan, top with the butter and cook in the oven at 350°F (180°C), Gas Mark 4 for 1 hour, basting with melted butter.

Serve the rabbit with the pan juices poured over it, accompanied by roast potatoes and a green salad.

Serves 4

PICCALILLI

We can thank the traders of the East India Company for this famous preserve. One recipe from 1694, headed 'To pickle lila, an Indian pickle', was clearly a vinegar-based sauce flavoured with spices in which were chunks of fruit and vegetables. That is still a fair description of the substance we call 'mustard pickle'.

2 lb mixed vegetables (green tomatoes, onions,
   cauliflower, cucumber, marrow, radish pods,
   nasturtium seeds, etc)
salt
1 tablespoon dry mustard (e.g. Colman's)
½ oz each of turmeric, ground ginger, flour
1 pint white vinegar
½ teaspoon celery seed

Chop the vegetables into small pieces (small onions, radish pods and nasturtium seeds can be left whole). Put into a bowl, sprinkle with salt and leave overnight. Next day wash free of salt and drain well. Then mix the mustard, spices and flour together with a little vinegar until you have a smooth paste; add the rest of the vinegar and the celery seeds and cook for 15 minutes until the sauce is thick. Pack the vegetables into jars and cover with the mustard mixture. Seal the jars.

For a sweet version, add 2 oz brown sugar to every pint of vinegar when making the sauce.

Makes 2-3 lbs

MUSTARD SAUCES

Variations on the theme of mustard sauce appear in many countries. Here are four versions using different mustards.

ENGLISH MUSTARD SAUCE

The classic accompaniment for rich, fatty fish like herrings. In the Middle Ages, cooks would 'lay' mustard over red herrings (heavily salted and smoked), but nowadays we tend to use it with grilled fresh herrings or herrings rolled in oatmeal. It also goes well with bloaters, grilled mackerel, poached cod, Finnan haddock and makes a splendid sauce for boiled salt beef and ham. It is also worth serving mustard sauce as an alternative to cheese sauce with vegetables such as cauliflower and fennel.

2 oz butter
2 oz flour
1 pint milk
2 teaspoons prepared English mustard (Colman's or Taylor's)
salt and pepper

Melt the butter in a saucepan and blend with the flour. Mix well and cook for 2 minutes. Remove from the heat and add a little milk, stirring continuously. Return to the heat, stir in the rest of the milk and cook gently for about 10 minutes. Add the mustard, adjust the seasoning and serve.

DANISH MUSTARD SAUCE

This cold sauce, enriched with cream, goes well with lobster, prawns and salmon, and makes an ideal garnish for open sandwiches.

1 hard-boiled egg yolk
1 raw egg yolk
2 teaspoons mild mustard (e.g. Slotts)
1 tablespoon white wine vinegar
salt and pepper
8 fl oz whipped double cream

Blend the egg yolks, mustard and wine vinegar. Add salt and pepper to taste. Gradually fold in the whipped cream and serve immediately.

GREEK MUSTARD SAUCE

A mustard and lemon sauce from a country not noted for its use of mustard. This cold sauce is almost akin to a vinaigrette and is served with egg and fish dishes.

4 cloves garlic
8 tablespoons olive oil
1 teaspoon dry mustard (e.g. Urchfont Mild Fine-
   Ground)
juice of 2 lemons
chopped parsley, to garnish

Pound the garlic, olive oil and mustard in a mortar. Add to the lemon juice. Stir well and garnish with chopped parsley before serving.

FRENCH MUSTARD SAUCE

Made from egg yolks, butter and mustard, this sauce is simplicity itself and, as Elizabeth David points out, its virtue is that fresh herbs can be added to suit what the sauce is to go with, e.g. fennel for fish, mint for lamb cutlets, tarragon for steak and chicken.

2 egg yolks
salt and pepper
1 teaspoon Dijon mustard
a few drops of tarragon vinegar
1 teaspoon fresh herbs, finely chopped
2 oz butter

Beat the egg yolks in a bowl, season and stir in the mustard, tarragon vinegar and fresh herbs. Melt the butter in a pan over hot water and, before it gets hot, add to the egg mixture, stirring until the sauce has the consistency of mayonnaise. Serve separately in a sauce boat.

MUSTARD IN MAYONNAISE

A teaspoon of Dijon mustard whisked with the egg yolks before adding the oil will improve mayonnaise and, once again, help to emulsify it. If the mayonnaise subsequently curdles or 'breaks', the mixture can be saved by beating it gradually into a teaspoon of Dijon mustard in a warm bowl. The secret is to go carefully, adding the mayonnaise drop by drop, and beating all the time.

MUSTARD IN VINAIGRETTE

Simple vinaigrette dressings are greatly improved by the addition of a little mustard, and the best to use is pale, fine-flavoured Dijon mustard such as Grey-Poupon. (Do not use dry mustard powder unless you want a mild, bitter flavour.)

Use the standard formula (1 part vinegar to 3 parts oil), and whisk together 1 teaspoon of mustard with 1 tablespoon of wine vinegar before adding the oil. The emulsifying properties of mustard help to prevent the dressing from separating.

Mustard vinaigrette is particularly good with strongly flavoured green salads like sorrel or dandelion leaves.

SOME QUICK IDEAS

BARBECUE SAUCE FOR SAUSAGES

William Tullberg recommends a throat-tingling mixture consisting of a dessertspoon of Urchfont mustard (try the Full Strength if you're fearless) with a little oil, vinegar and Worcestershire sauce, which is brushed over the sausages during cooking.

MUSTARD BUTTER

Take 2 oz of creamed butter and blend in 2-3 teaspoons of smooth Dijon mustard (e.g. Grey-Poupon); or for an unusual speckled appearance use coarse-grained Amora or Maille. Form into a block, chill and serve a slice on grilled steaks or fish.

ANCHOVY MUSTARD

Chop and pound 8 anchovy fillets and mix with 6 oz strong English mustard (e.g. Colman's or Taylor's). Store in a covered pot. This combination is nothing new, in fact Mrs Beeton's so-called Indian Mustard had anchovy sauce as one of its ingredients, and Jesuits' Mustard was also based on fish. (See page 9.)

MUSTARD WITH KIPPERS

A personal favourite. Bone a freshly grilled kipper and spread with a little mustard. Choose the mustard to suit the fish: the sweetest, most delicate Manx kippers deserve the sharp, subtle flavour of *Moutarde de Meaux,* while meaty Loch Fyne kippers can cope with something more robust, like Gordon's Vineyard Mustard.

A Dip For German Sausages

Mix 2 teaspoons of German mustard with a small carton of plain natural yoghurt; add a teaspoon each of finely chopped onion and pickled gherkin. Sprinkle with fresh parsley. Serve with hot frankfurters, bratwurst and bockwurst.

A Coating For Lamb Cutlets

Spread cutlets with the mustard of your choice, dip in egg and coat in breadcrumbs. Fry in oil until brown all over. Also useful for veal escalopes, pig's trotters, etc.

A Glaze For Ham

Remove the skin from boiled ham and coat the meat with a mixture of 1 tablespoon Dijon mustard, 1 heaped tablespoon redcurrant jelly, juice of 1 orange and 1 dessertspoon of brown sugar blended to a thick paste. Put the ham in the oven for about 20 minutes at 400°F (200°C), Gas Mark 6, and baste well.

A Glaze For Carrots

Mix together 1 tablespoon of honey, 1 tablespoon of butter and 2 teaspoons of Dijon mustard and blend over a low heat. Use to glaze freshly cooked and drained carrots.

USES OF WHOLE MUSTARD SEED

As well as providing the raw material for prepared mustards, whole mustard seeds can also be used on their own.

White mustard seed, because of its preservative powers, is an important ingredient of pickling spice (along with coriander seeds, chillies, cloves, ginger, allspice, etc) and can be used in this form for a whole range of preserves. It also appears in some chutney recipes. It can be sprinkled over salt pork, beef or bacon during boiling; mixed into potato salad to add an element of crunchiness; tossed with steamed cabbage and used as a garnish for fish, veal and chicken dishes.

Black mustard seed is very common in Indian cooking. As well as appearing in pickles and preserves, the seeds are roasted in hot fat or ghee until they begin to splutter, and used as a garnish particularly for vegetarian dishes. The effect is pleasantly nutty rather than pungent.

The Japanese stuff porous lotus roots with black mustard seeds and serve them deep-fried in paper-thin batter as tempura.

Mustard Seed Recipes
Lemon And Mustard Seed Chutney

A sharp, fiery chutney made from white mustard seed.

4 large lemons
8 oz onions
1 oz salt
1 pint cider vinegar
4 oz sultanas
1 oz white mustard seed
1 teaspoon ground ginger
1 teaspoon cayenne pepper
1 lb white sugar

Wipe the lemons with a damp cloth and chop finely, removing the pips. Peel and chop onions and put them in a bowl with the lemons. Sprinkle with salt and leave overnight. Next day put the contents of the bowl into a pan and simmer with a little water until soft. Add the cider vinegar, sultanas, spices and sugar; bring to the boil and continue to simmer for about 30 minutes until thick. Then spoon into warm jars and cover.

Makes 2-3 lbs chutney

MAHANI

This marvellous Punjabi dish combines the earthiness of lentils with the bewitching perfume of mangoes. For the best results use *channa dhal* (large yellow grains rather like translucent split peas).

8 oz lentils, washed well
1 pint water or good stock
1 teaspoon turmeric
3 large ripe mangoes
salt to taste
1 teaspoon black mustard seeds
1 teaspoon cumin seeds
½ teaspoon kalonji (black onion
  seeds) (optional)
2 tablespoons ghee or cooking oil

Soak lentils in water overnight. Next day cook them in 1 pint water or good stock with the turmeric. Season with salt when almost cooked.

Meanwhile cut open the mangoes, remove the stones and squeeze out the juice. Add this to the lentils when they have absorbed most of the water. Simmer for 10-15 minutes. Transfer the lentils to a serving dish.

Fry the mustard seeds, cumin seeds and kalonji in hot ghee or oil until they splutter. Then sprinkle them over the lentils. Eat with boiled rice or as a side dish with chicken.

Serves 4

MUSTARD OIL

This is a very useful 'fatty' oil obtained by pressing the seeds of all three mustard plants, as well as those of field mustard *(Brassica campestris)*, rape *(Brassica napus)* and even turnips *(Brassica rapa)*. It is very important in India, Pakistan, Sri Lanka and parts of South-East Asia, which together account for nearly half the world's production.

The virtues of this distinctive oil were extolled by no lesser person than Mahatma Gandhi, who noted that as well as 98 to 99 per cent fat, it also contained valuable trace elements such as manganese and cobalt. He also claimed that if it was rubbed on the skin it helped the production of Vitamin D through the agency of sunlight. Bengali mothers had been doing just that for centuries, rubbing their babies with mustard oil and putting them out in the sun to brown!

Mustard oil is used for cooking fish, and in a wide range of pickles, from whole mangoes and stuffed red chillies (which would keep for at least two years) to pheasant and partridge. It provides flavour and acts as an air-excluding preservative.

It was also the custom to fumigate pickling jars by sprinkling a few drops of mustard oil over red-hot charcoal and allowing the fumes to circulate inside the upturned containers. Then a paste of salt and mustard oil was spread on for added protection.

Mustard oil is also a vital ingredient of *mostarda di Cremona,* a remarkable Italian product.

MOSTARDA DI CREMONA

This curious confection—half conserve, half condiment—is a speciality of Northern Italy, and is obviously a survivor from the past, when elaborate preserves were the order of the day. It was recorded in the 17th century by the English diarist John Evelyn (who also wrote *Acetaria*, a fascinating little book on herbs and salad vegetables); he noted that the Italians made a condiment by mixing orange and lemon peel with black mustard seed.

Mostarda di Cremona (or *mostarda di frutta*) is still prepared today from whole fruits such as pears, cherries, figs, plums, apricots and slices of melon and pumpkin, all preserved in thick syrup with mustard oil. It is a unique and quite splendid substance, exquisite to look at and equally delicious as a kind of sweetmeat or as a condiment to go with cold tongue, pork or ham. In Northern Italy it is traditionally eaten with eels roasted on a spit, but perhaps the most bizarre recipe of all is Marinetti's in his book *Futurist Cooking* (1932): he recommends steeping a whole roasted pheasant in heavy Sicilian muscat wine, then bathing it in milk, and finally stuffing it with *mostarda* and candied fruit.

In Italy, *mostarda* is sold from big wooden pails, but in this country you will find it on the shelves of good Italian delicatessens in clear glass jars.

MUSTARD CURES

Greek physicians like Hippocrates were familiar with the curative and therapeutic uses of mustard. They administered the seeds internally, and used them for poultices made with vinegar.

The influential English herbalists of the 16th and 17th centuries all had something good to say about mustard, and praised its many virtues. (However, it was not until the *London Pharmacopoeia* of 1720 that any distinction was made between black and white mustard.) Herbal remedies, like recipes, are perpetuated and passed on from one writer to another, so there tends to be a great deal of duplication. But here are some of the attributes of mustard as seen by the herbal wizards. To begin with, a note from John Parkinson, who believed that mustard was 'of good use for Epileticke persons, if it be applied hot inwardly and outwardly'.

John Gerard, in his *Herbal* of 1597, cleverly brought together the culinary and therapeutic usefulness of mustard: 'the seede of Mustarde', he said, 'pounded with vinegar is an excellent sauce, good to be eaten with any grosse meates, either fish or flesh, because it doth help digestion, warmeth the stomache and provoketh appetite'. Sound advice, indeed. But that was not all. Mustard was given for those who were 'short winded and stopped in the breath'; it helped toothache 'if chewed in the mouth'; with honey and vinegar it made 'a gargarisme against the swellings and almonds about the throat and the root of the tongue'; not surprisingly it caused sneezing if put into the nostrils; it was mixed with good success with drawing plasters, and apparently was of benefit to persons that had their hair pulled off; it was also 'good against the falling sickness and such that have lithargie, if it be laid plasterwise upon the head (after shaving) being tempered with figs'.

Nicholas Culpeper did even better in *The Complete Herbal* (1653). As well as echoing many of Gerard's remarks, he claimed that mustard was good against snake poison 'if taken in time', that 'a decoction of the seeds resists the malignity of mushrooms', and that balls of honey and mustard taken every morning during fasting would 'clear the voice' and banish 'that drowsy forgetful evil'. It would also help a crick in the neck and dispel bruises!

Much of this wisdom still held good in the 19th century, if the advertising for Colman's mustard plasters is anything to go by. 'It purges the body of toxic products, relieving pain, giving a feeling of warmth and well-being, and an increased flow of blood; it stimulates capillary circulation, relieves rheumatism, colds, 'flu, bronchitis, coughs on the chest, aches in the nape of the neck, neuralgia in the side of the face, and toothache.' How the old herbalists would have applauded that testimony!

These days we still make use of mustard as a medicine, although our language is different and we have the benefit of scientific explanations to throw light on the subject. An infusion of white mustard seeds can be used to relieve the effects of chronic bronchitis, and mustard seed tea can soothe a sore throat if gargled. White mustard is also a powerful preservative—hence its uses in pickling—and it is a keen troubleshooter against unfriendly bacteria. It is also an emulsifying agent, so it helps with the digestion of heavy fatty foods, holding fat globules in suspension until the bile can break them down. (Lovers of pork pies and fat, home-cured bacon, please note!)

Black mustard is variously an irritant, a stimulant, a diuretic (i.e. it promotes urine) and an emetic, depending on how you take it. Mustard poultices, applied externally near inflammation can help to relieve congestion by 'drawing forth', or drawing blood to the surface.

Then, of course, there are mustard baths. Exhausted Victorian huntsmen thought there was no

better tonic than a mustard bath for the feet and a large whisky for the inner man! And anyone who wants to throw off a cold or relieve aches and pains could do worse than make a bath by pouring boiling water on bruised mustard seed or even mustard powder. (The whisky is an optional extra!)

It is also claimed that mustard oil rubbed into the scalp promotes the growth of hair. So, it seems that the herbalists were right after all!

QUOTATIONS

'If he chanced to spit, it was whole basketsful of
   goldfinches.
If he blowed his nose, it was pickled grigs.
When he wept, it was ducks with onion sauce.
When he sneezed, it was whole tubfuls of mustard.
When he coughed, it was boxes of marmalade.
When he sobbed, it was watercresses . . .'

Rabelais, *Pantagruel*, 1584,
tr. Sir Thomas Urquart

' "Good folks", said Sancho, "my master does not
want you heartening; why do not you run in and
help him? Though I believe it is after-meat mustard;
for sure the giant is dead by this time." '

Cervantes, *Don Quixote*

'Amelia mixed the mustard,
   She mixed it good and thick;
She put it in the custard
   And made her Mother sick,
And showing satisfaction
   By many a loud huzza
"Observe," said she, "the action
   Of mustard on Mamma." '

A.E. Housman

'Tis ever thus with simple folk—an accepted wit has
but to say "Pass the mustard", and they roar their
ribs out.'

W.S. Gilbert, *The Yeomen of the Guard*

'Good husband and huswife now chiefly be glad,
things handsome to have as they ought to be had.
They do provide, against Christmas do come,
to welcome their neighbours, good chere to have
    some.
Good bread and good drink, a good fier in the hall,
brawne, pudding and souse, and good mustarde
    withal.
Bief, mutton, and porke, and good pies of the best,
pig, veal, goose and capon, and turkey well drest.
Chese, apples, and nuttes, and good caroles to heare,
as then, in the country, is counted good chere.'

Thomas Tusser, *Christmas Husbandly Fare*
from *Five Hundred Points of
Good Husbandry*, 1580

ACKNOWLEDGEMENTS

I should like to thank the following for their advice,
help and encouragement during the writing of this
book.

William Tullberg, Wiltshire Tracklements
Charles Gordon, Charles Gordon Associates
Paul Parmenter, Colman's of Norwich
S.J. Taylor, Taylor's Mustard Ltd.
Food and Wine from France
The German Food Centre
The Danish Food Centre